30 Easy Spanish Guitar Solos

Arranged by Mark Phillips

Recording credits:
Guitar: Doug Boduch
Guitar made by Jim Mitchell, Milwaukee, WI

Cherry Lane Music Company
Director of Publications/Project Editor: Mark Phillips
Publications Coordinator: Gabrielle Fastman

ISBN: 978-1-60378-059-9

T0057390

Copyright © 2008 Cherry Lane Music Company
International Copyright Secured All Rights Reserved

The music, text, design and graphics in this publication are protected by copyright law. Any duplication or transmission, by any means, electronic, mechanical, photocopying, recording or otherwise, is an infringement of copyright.

Visit Hal Leonard Online at
www.halleonard.com

CONTENTS

4 A la Nanita Nana

3 Adelita

6 Cielito Lindo

10 Ejercicio in E Minor

8 Ejercicio No. 10/9

13 El Cascabel

16 El Choclo

18 El Humahuaqueño

20 El Noi de la Mare

21 Fantasia in E Minor (Les Adieux)

24 Farruca

26 Gerbe des Fleurs

28 Habemos Llegado

29 La Borinqueña

32 La Llorona

34 La Paloma

36 La Zandunga

38 Lagrima

40 Leyenda

42 Malagueña

44 Mi Caballo Blanco

46 Mi Hamaca

48 Molondrón

50 Roman Castillo

52 Romanza

56 Salamanca

58 Tango No. 3

55 Tres Hojitas, Madre

60 Una Tarde Fresquita de Mayo

62 Villanesca

Adelita

By Francisco Tarrega

This Arrangement Copyright © 2008 Cherry Lane Music Company
International Copyright Secured All Rights Reserved

A la Nanita Nana

Traditional

This Arrangement Copyright © 2008 Cherry Lane Music Company
International Copyright Secured All Rights Reserved

¢II
1.
2.

Cielito Lindo

Traditional

This Arrangement Copyright © 2008 Cherry Lane Music Company
International Copyright Secured All Rights Reserved

¢II
1.
2.
Harm.

Ejercicio No. 10/9

By Jose Ferrer

This Arrangement Copyright © 2008 Cherry Lane Music Company
International Copyright Secured All Rights Reserved

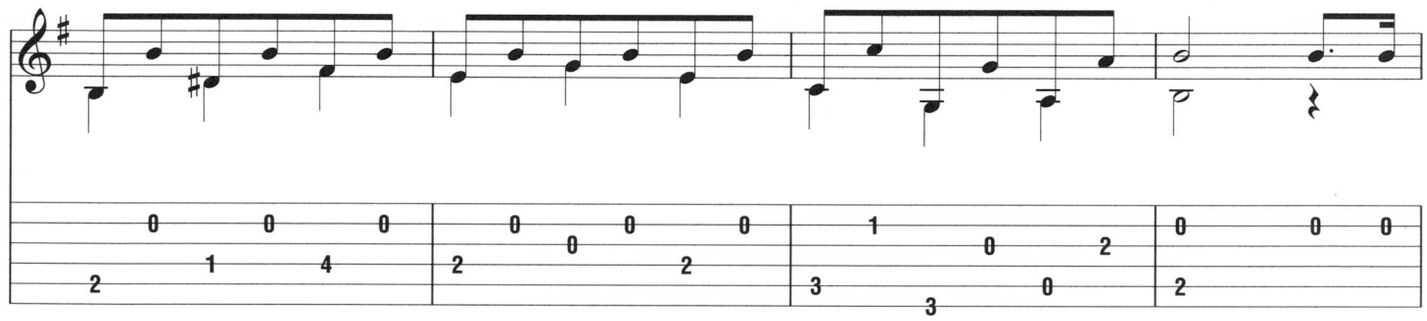

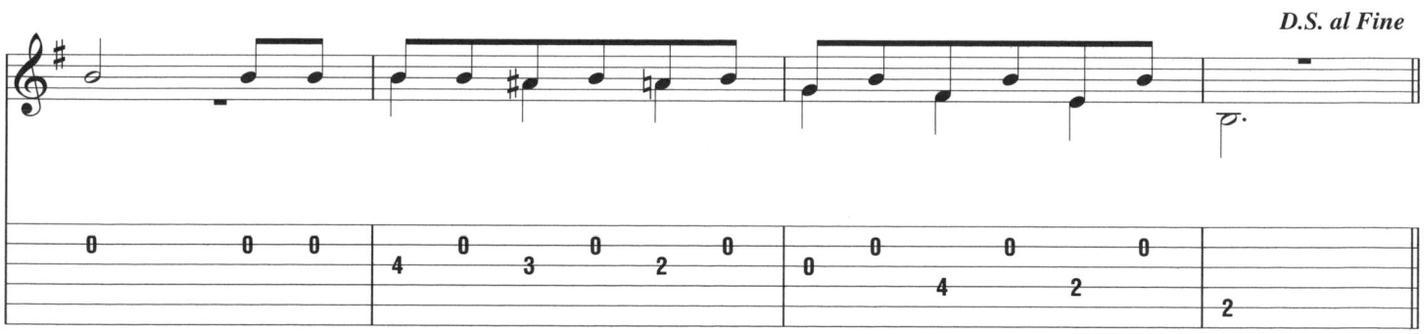
D.S. al Fine

Ejercicio in E Minor

By Jose Ferrer

This Arrangement Copyright © 2008 Cherry Lane Music Company
International Copyright Secured All Rights Reserved

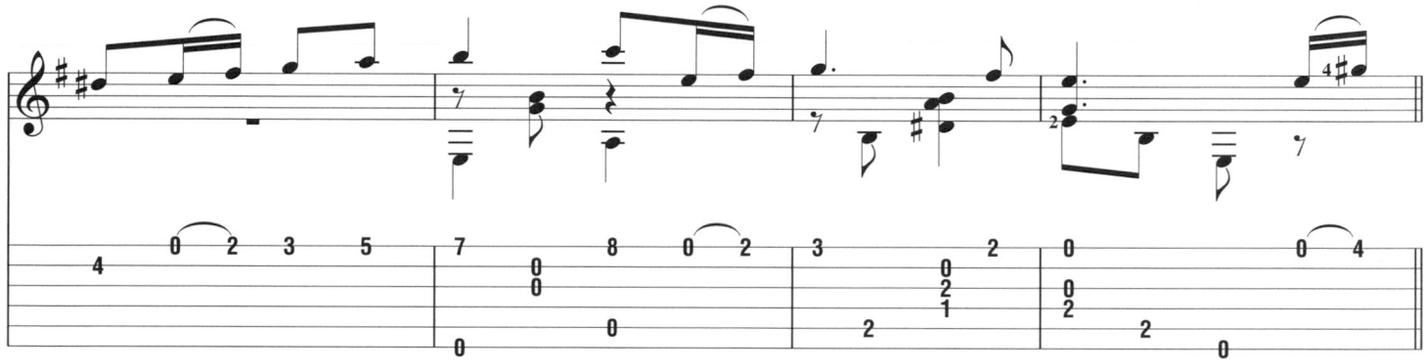

¢V
¢V

Harm.

El Cascabel

Traditional

This Arrangement Copyright © 2008 Cherry Lane Music Company
International Copyright Secured All Rights Reserved

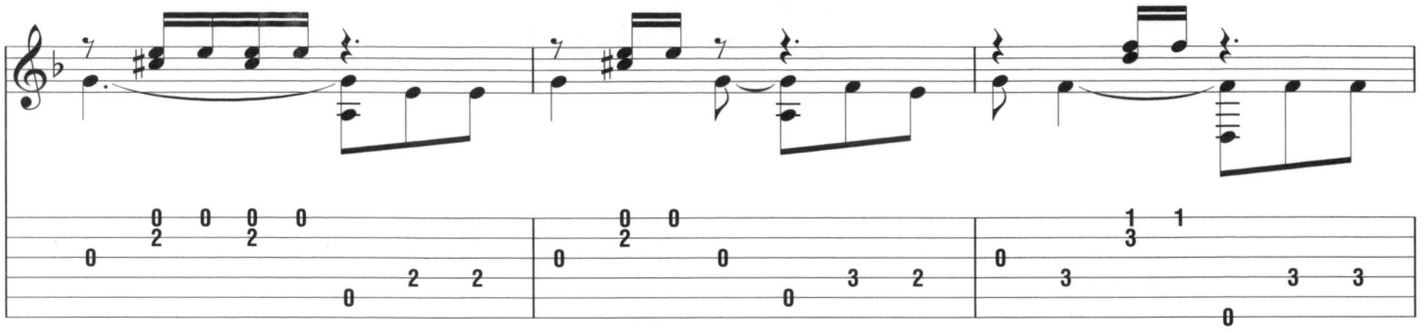

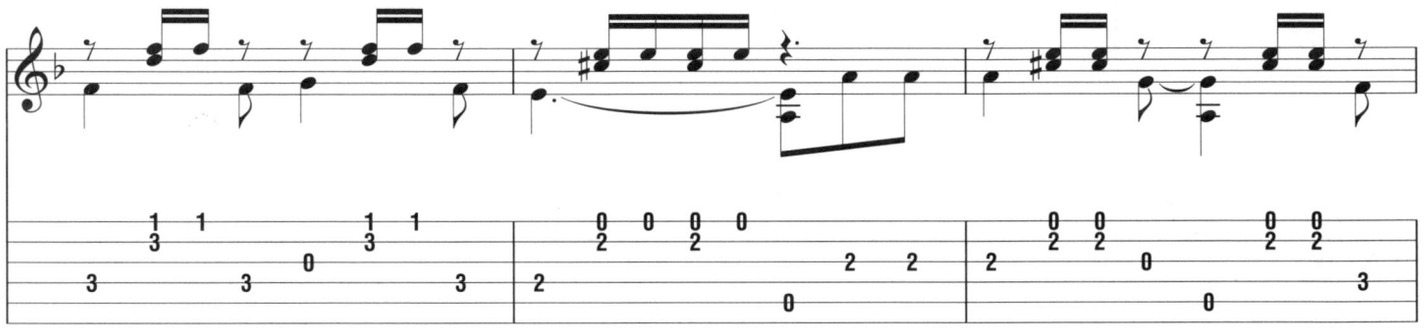

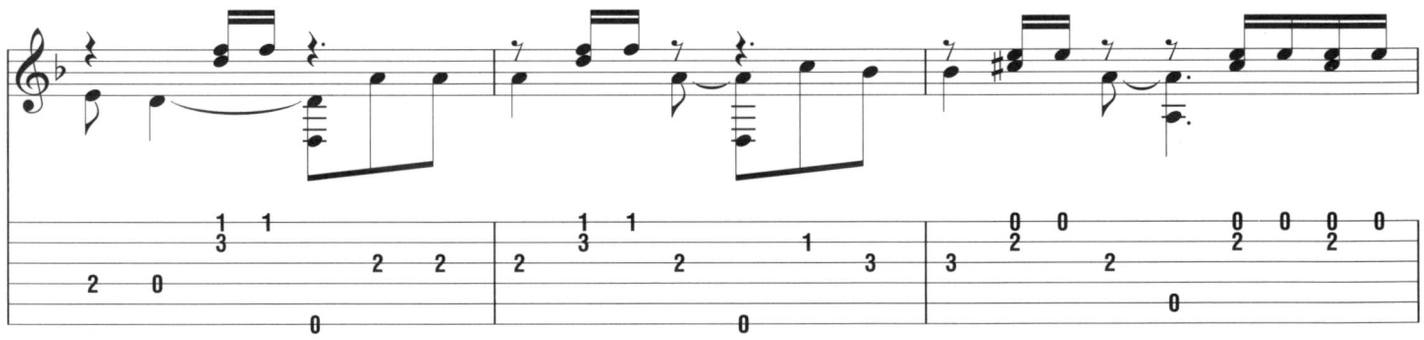

El Choclo

By Angel Villoldo

This Arrangement Copyright © 2008 Cherry Lane Music Company
International Copyright Secured All Rights Reserved

1.
2.

El Humahuaqueño

Traditional

This Arrangement Copyright © 2008 Cherry Lane Music Company
International Copyright Secured All Rights Reserved

Last time to Coda
1.
2.
D.S. al Coda
(with repeats)
Coda
m
i
m

El Noi de la Mare

Traditional

This Arrangement Copyright © 2008 Cherry Lane Music Company
International Copyright Secured All Rights Reserved

Fantasia in E Minor
(Les Adieux)

By Fernando Sor

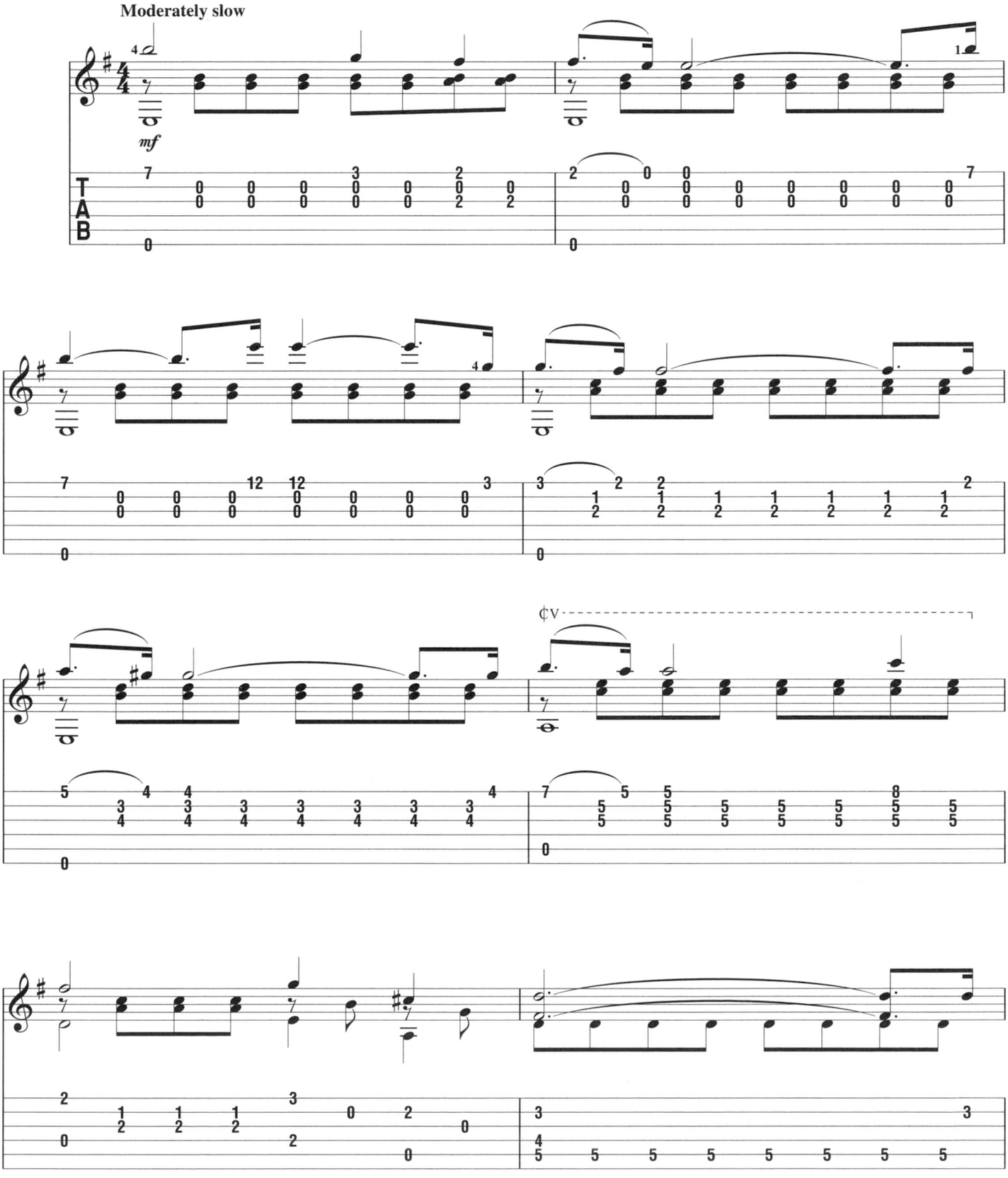

This Arrangement Copyright © 2008 Cherry Lane Music Company
International Copyright Secured All Rights Reserved

¢VI
¢VII
¢VIII
¢VII
¢VII
¢V
¢III
¢III

Moderately fast
¢V
¢II
¢II

Farruca

Traditional

This Arrangement Copyright © 2008 Cherry Lane Music Company
International Copyright Secured All Rights Reserved

i
p
i
p
m
i
m
p
m
i
m
p
m
i
m
p

Gerbe des Fleurs

By Jose Ferrer

This Arrangement Copyright © 2007 Cherry Lane Music Company
International Copyright Secured All Rights Reserved

¢VII
D.S. al Fine
(take 2nd ending)

Habemos Llegado

Traditional

This Arrangement Copyright © 2008 Cherry Lane Music Company
International Copyright Secured All Rights Reserved

La Borinqueña

Traditional

This Arrangement Copyright © 2008 Cherry Lane Music Company
International Copyright Secured All Rights Reserved

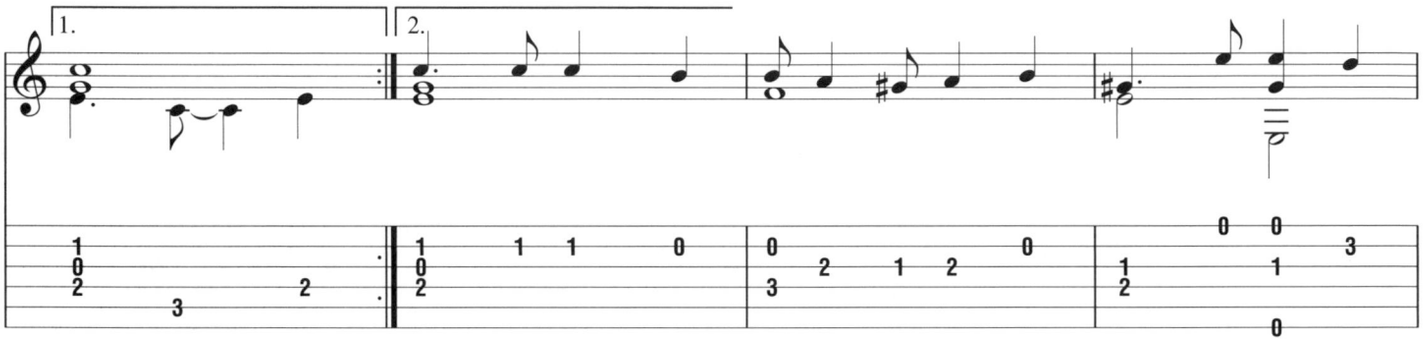
1.
2.

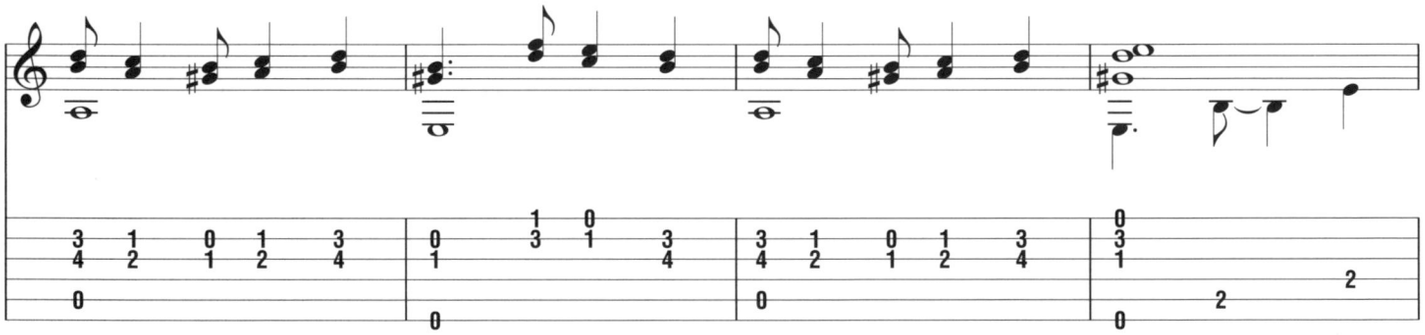

CII
1.
2.
¢II

La Llorona

Traditional

This Arrangement Copyright © 2008 Cherry Lane Music Company
International Copyright Secured All Rights Reserved

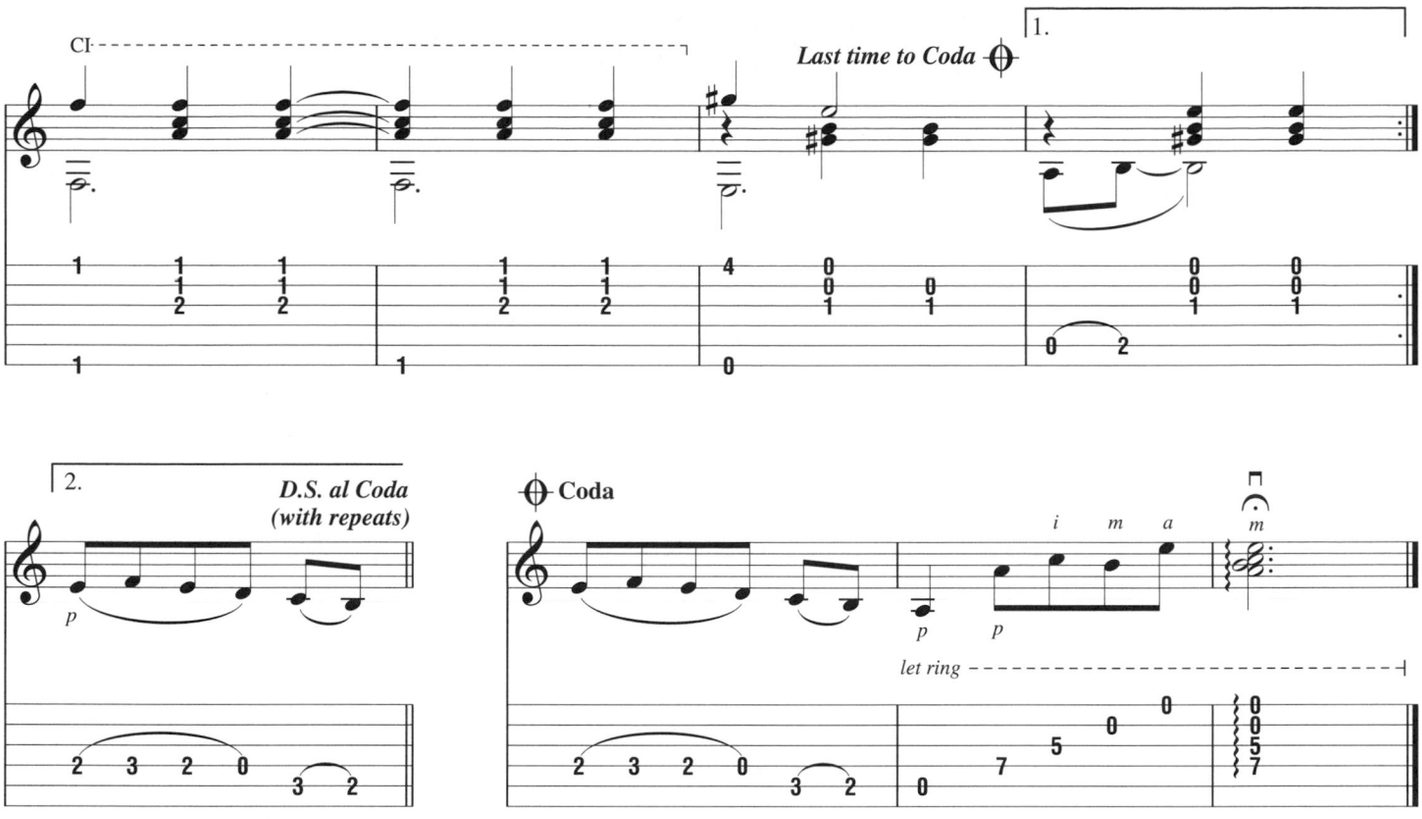
CI
Last time to Coda
1.
2.
D.S. al Coda
(with repeats)
p
Coda
i m a
m
p
p
let ring

La Paloma

By Sebastian Yradier

This Arrangement Copyright © 2008 Cherry Lane Music Company
International Copyright Secured All Rights Reserved

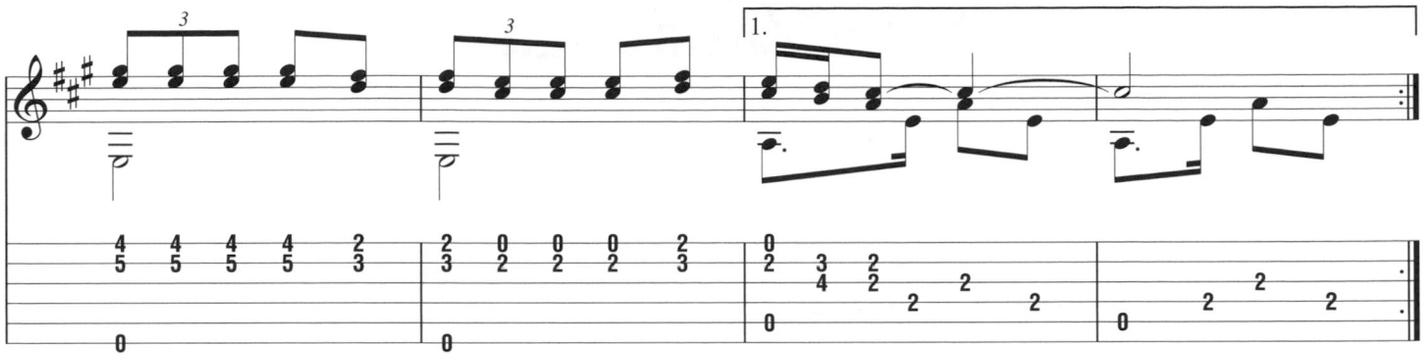
1.

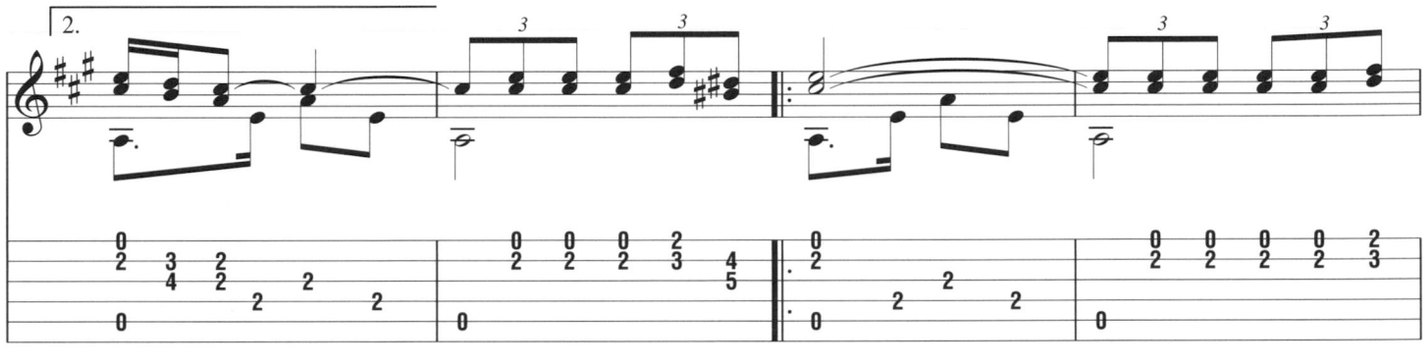
2.

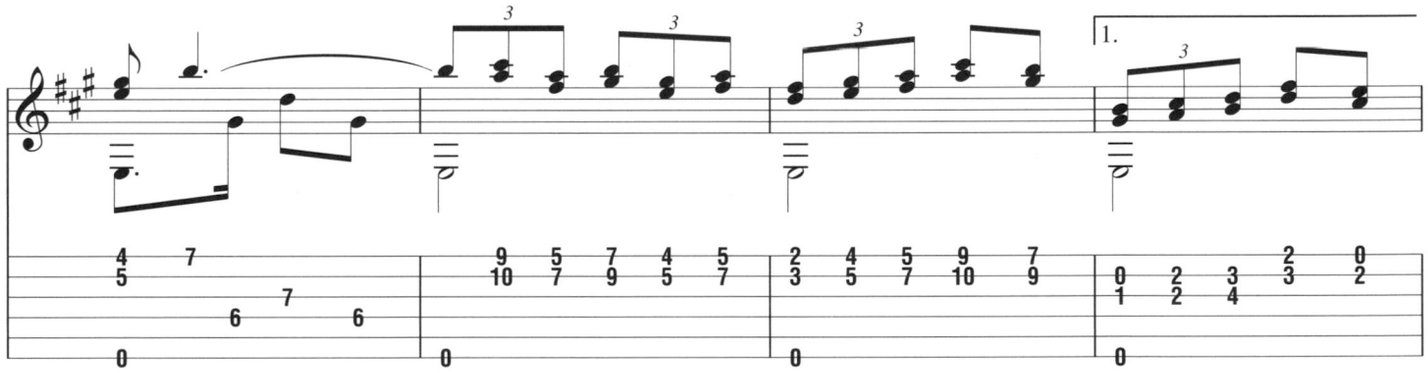
1.

2.
Harm.

La Zandunga

Traditional

This Arrangement Copyright © 2008 Cherry Lane Music Company
International Copyright Secured All Rights Reserved

D.S. al Coda
Coda

Lagrima

By Francisco Tarrega

This Arrangement Copyright © 2007 Cherry Lane Music Company
International Copyright Secured All Rights Reserved

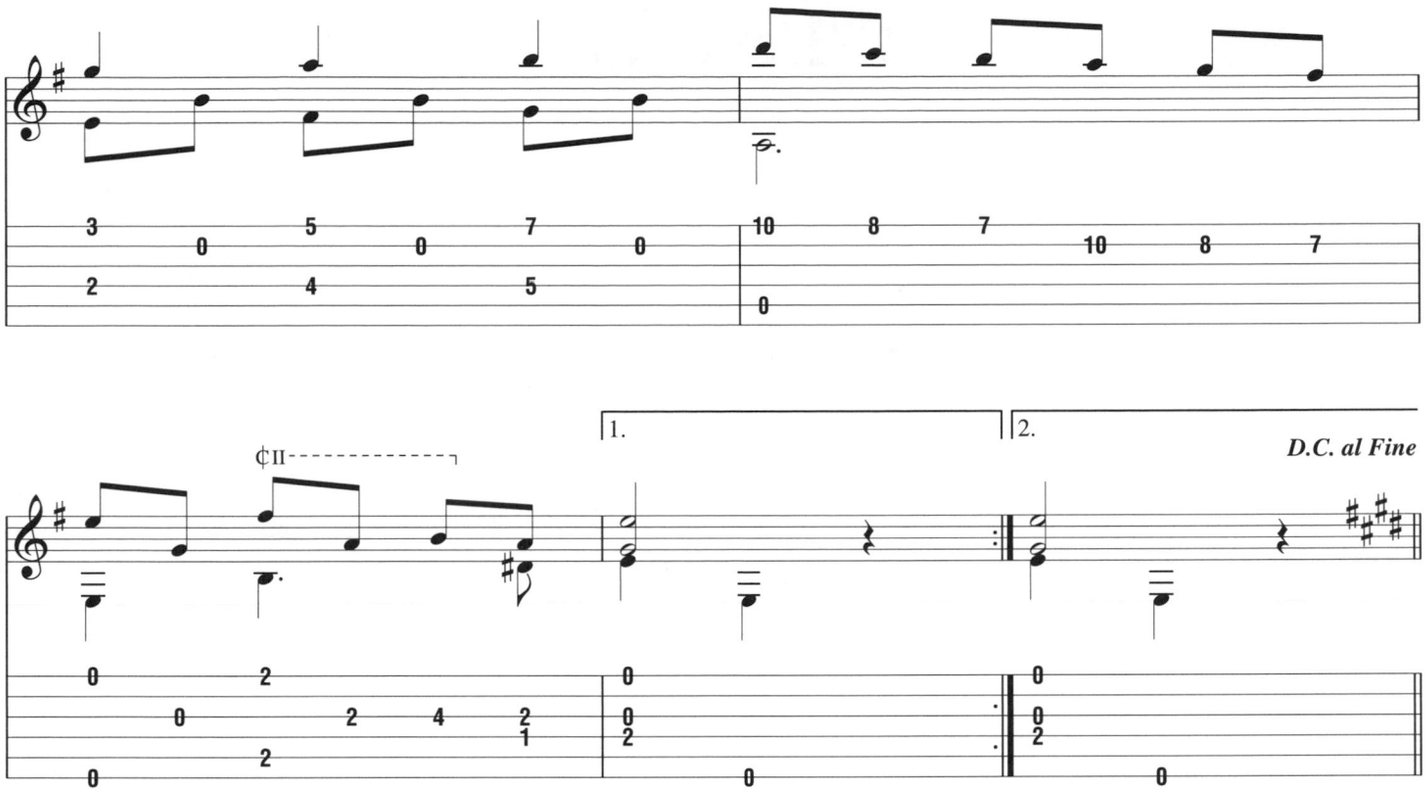
1.
2.
D.C. al Fine

Leyenda

By Isaac Albeniz

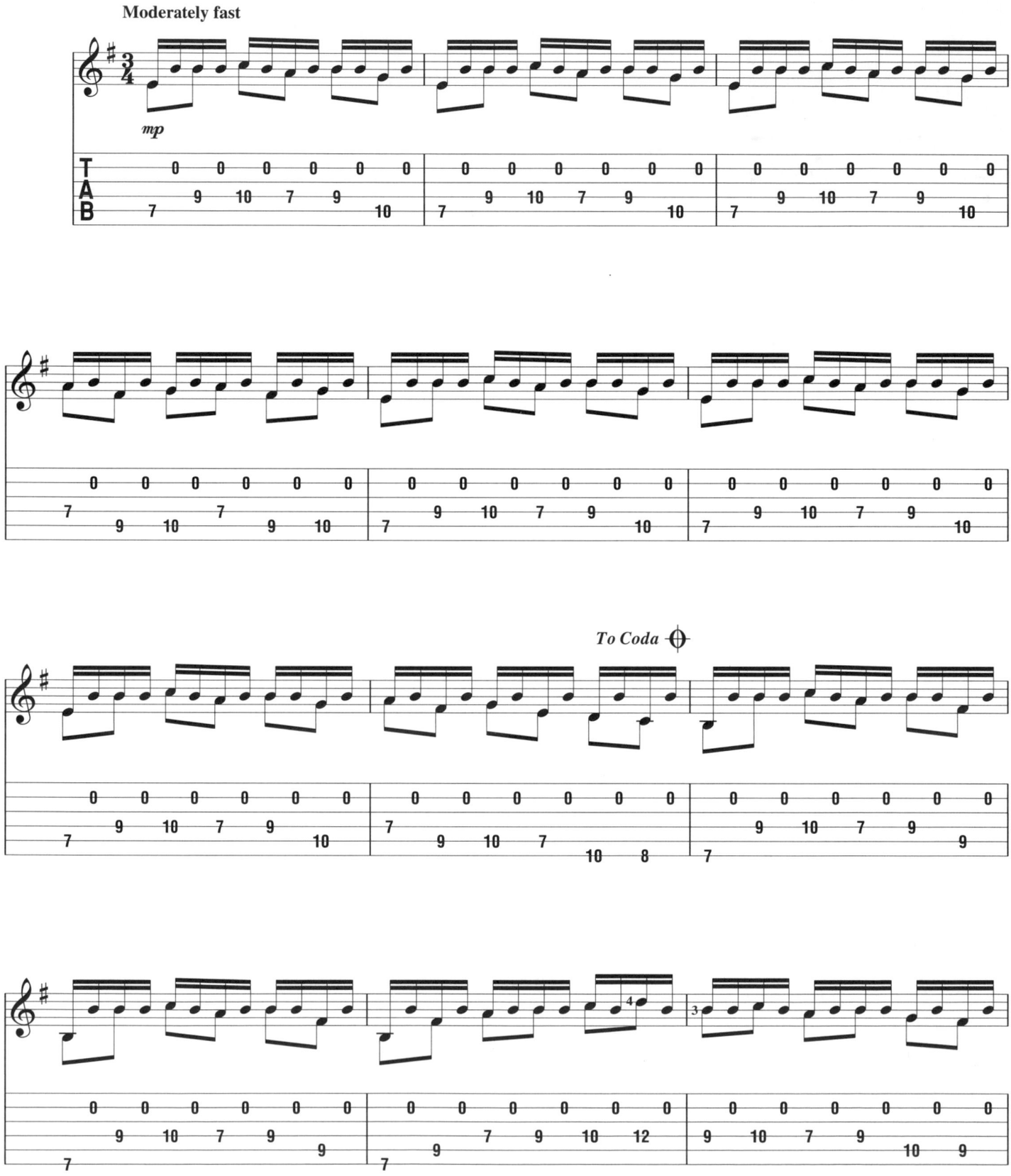

This Arrangement Copyright © 2008 Cherry Lane Music Company
International Copyright Secured All Rights Reserved

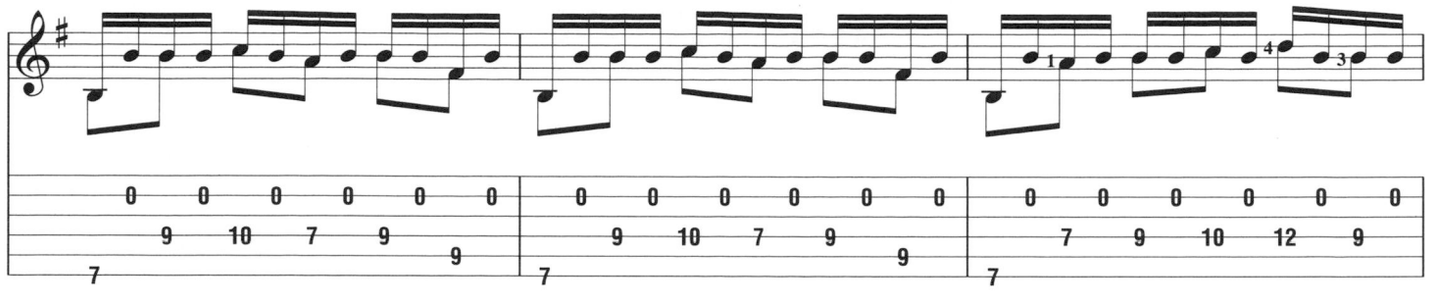

D.C. al Coda

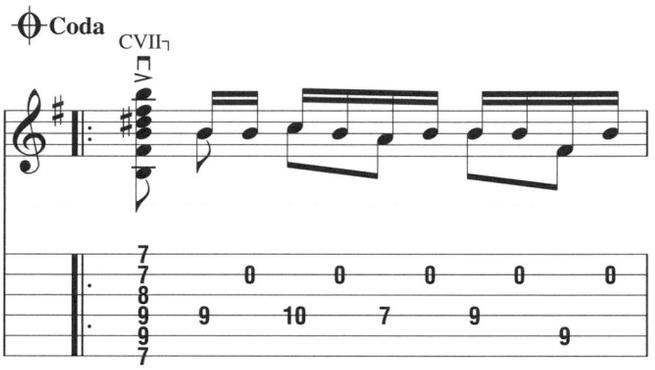
Coda
CVII

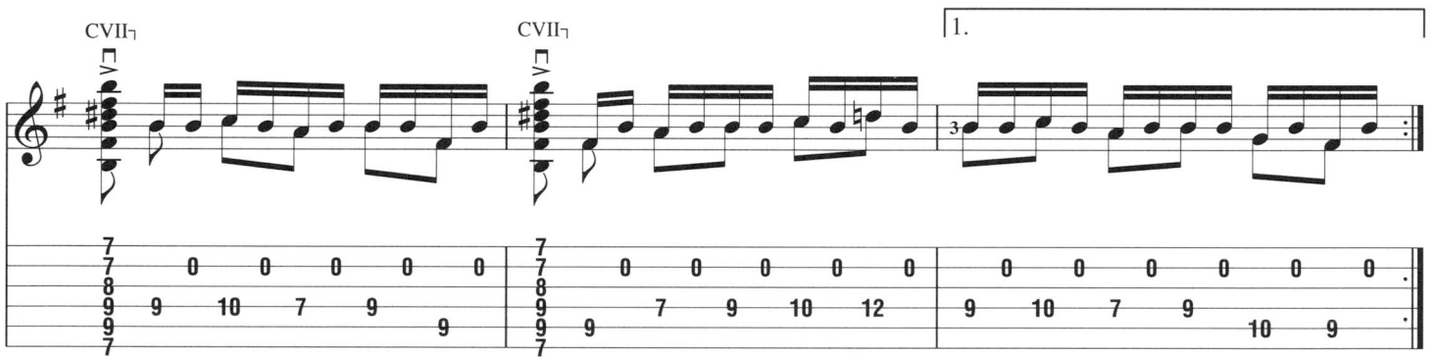
CVII
CVII
1.

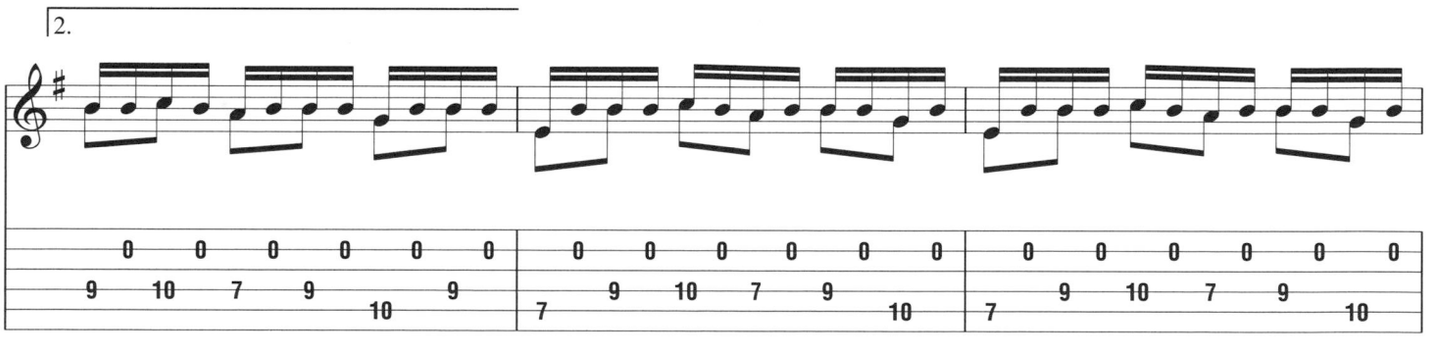
2.

rit. e dim.
p

Malagueña

By Francisco Tarrega

This Arrangement Copyright © 2008 Cherry Lane Music Company
International Copyright Secured All Rights Reserved

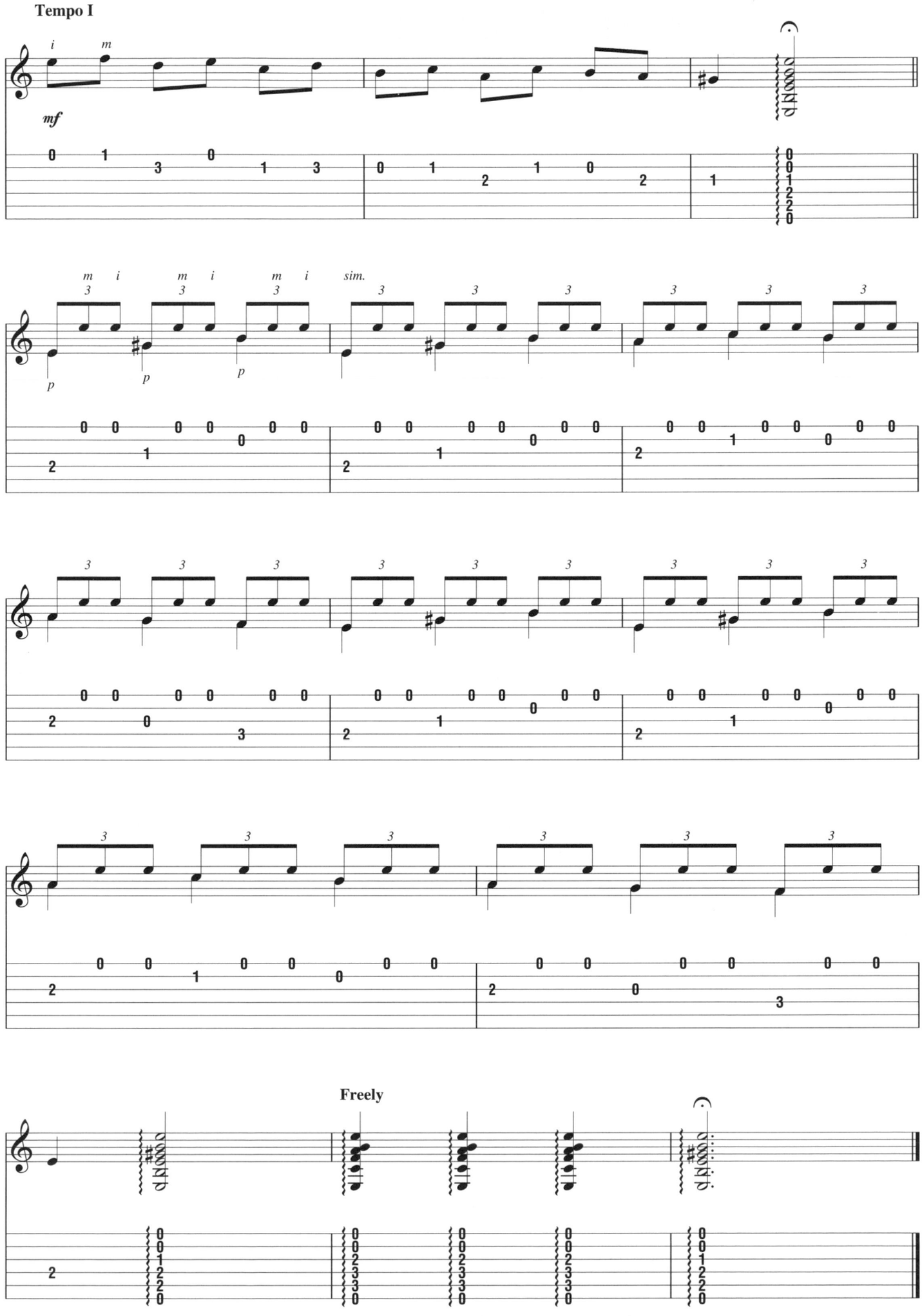
Tempo I
i m
mf
m i m i m i sim.
p p p
Freely

Mi Caballo Blanco

Traditional

This Arrangement Copyright © 2008 Cherry Lane Music Company
International Copyright Secured All Rights Reserved

1.
2.

Mi Hamaca

Traditional

This Arrangement Copyright © 2008 Cherry Lane Music Company
International Copyright Secured All Rights Reserved

Molondrón

Traditional

This Arrangement Copyright © 2008 Cherry Lane Music Company
International Copyright Secured All Rights Reserved

1.
2.
Harm.

Roman Castillo

Traditional

This Arrangement Copyright © 2008 Cherry Lane Music Company
International Copyright Secured All Rights Reserved

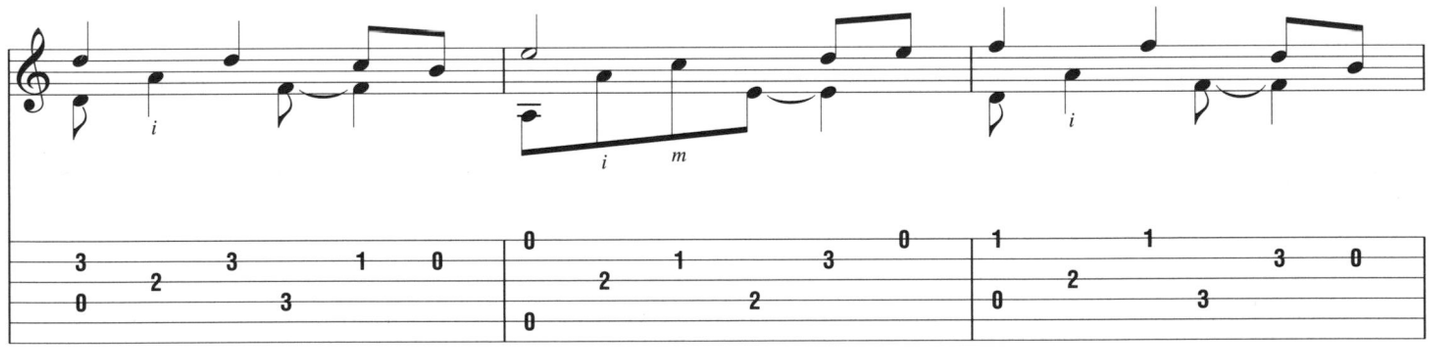

1.
2.

Romanza

Anonymous

This Arrangement Copyright © 2008 Cherry Lane Music Company
International Copyright Secured All Rights Reserved

CVII
Fine
¢II

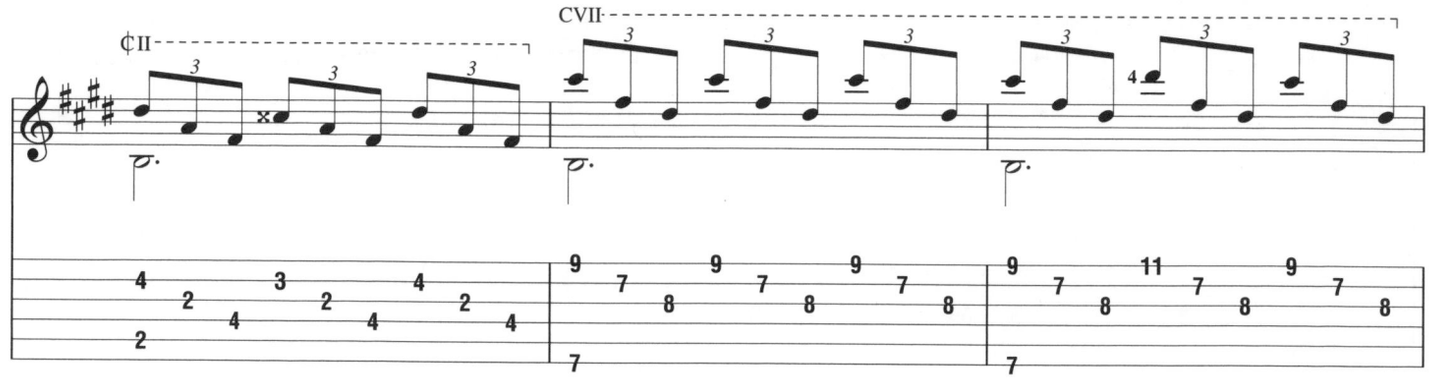
¢II
CVII

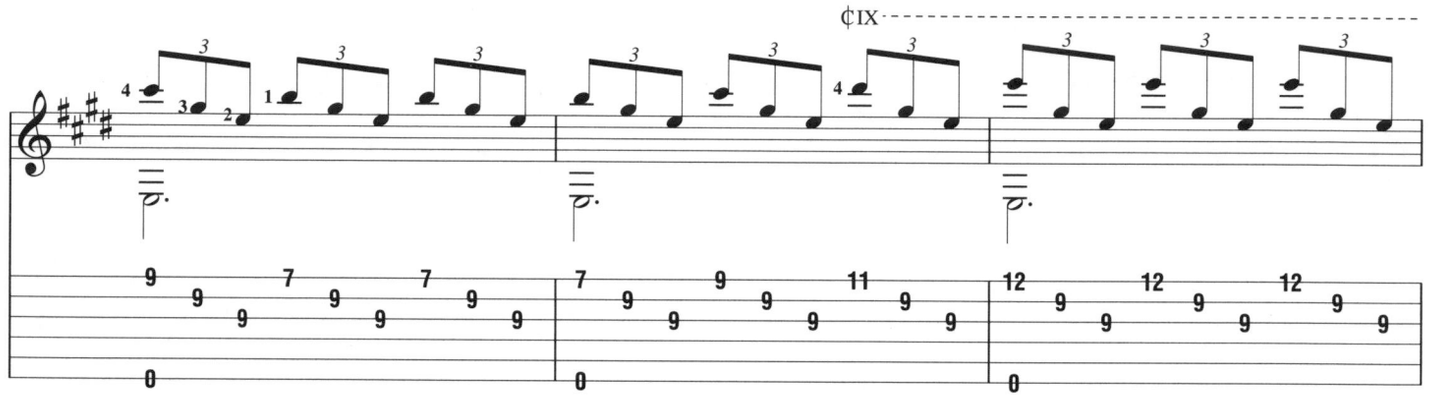
¢IX

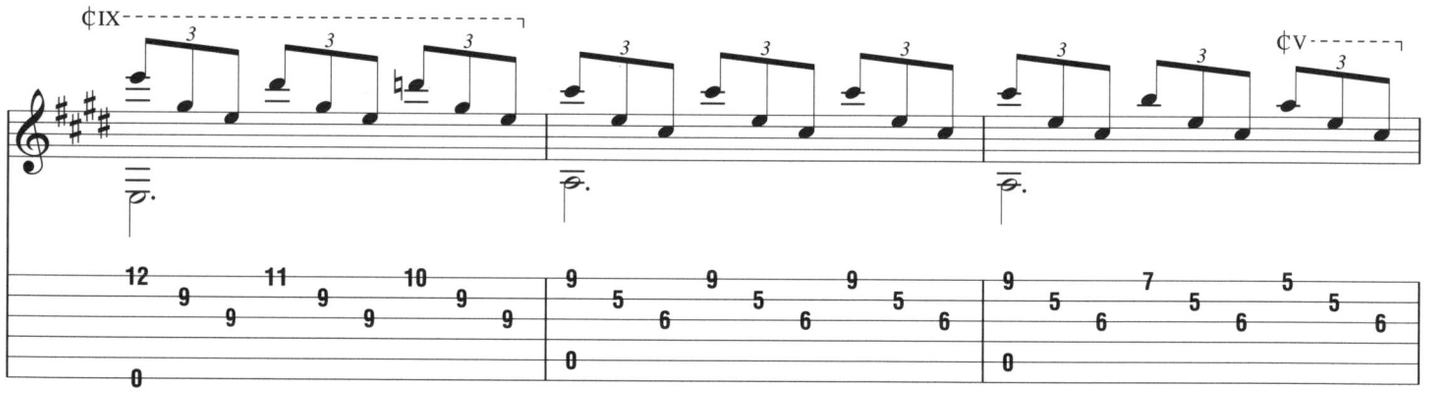
¢IX
¢V

¢II
D.C. al Fine

Tres Hojitas, Madre

Traditional

This Arrangement Copyright © 2008 Cherry Lane Music Company
International Copyright Secured All Rights Reserved

Salamanca

Traditional

This Arrangement Copyright © 2008 Cherry Lane Music Company
International Copyright Secured All Rights Reserved

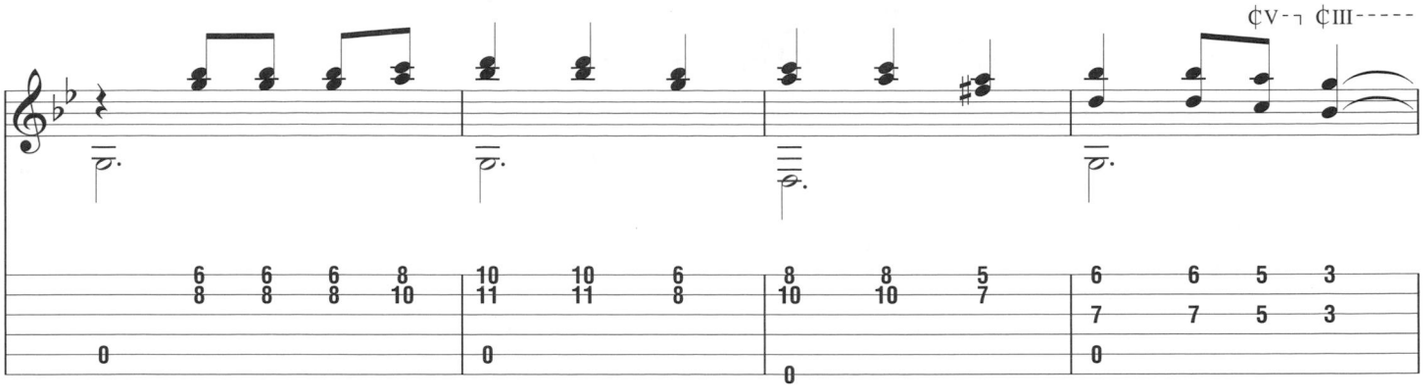
¢V
¢III

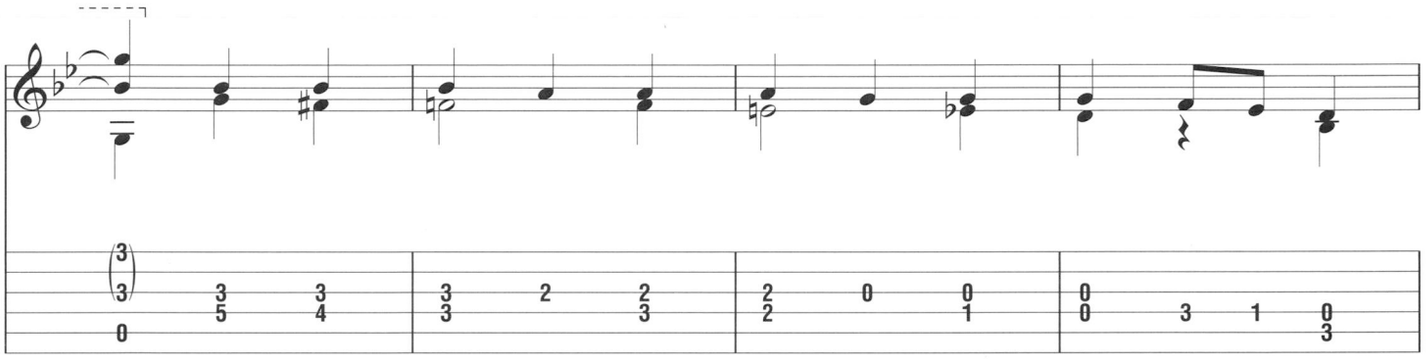

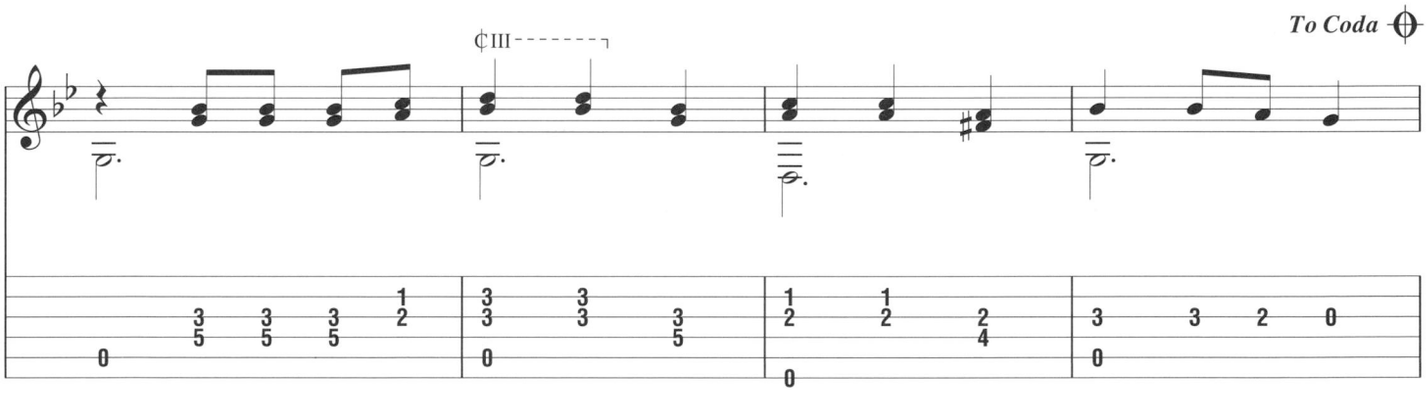
To Coda
¢III

D.S. al Coda
(with repeat)
¢XII
Harm.

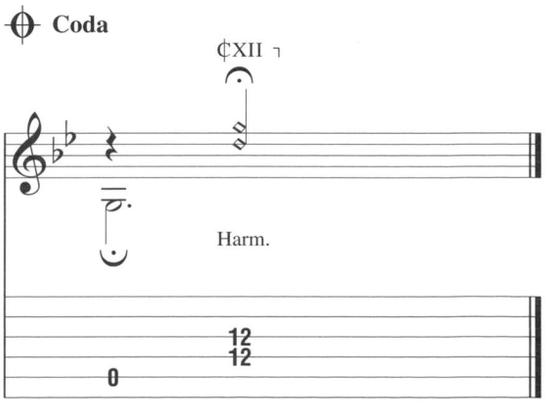
Coda
¢XII
Harm.

Tango No. 3

By Jose Ferrer

This Arrangement Copyright © 2008 Cherry Lane Music Company
International Copyright Secured All Rights Reserved

1.
2.
D.S. al Coda
(no repeat)
Coda

Una Tarde Fresquita de Mayo

Traditional

This Arrangement Copyright © 2008 Cherry Lane Music Company
International Copyright Secured All Rights Reserved

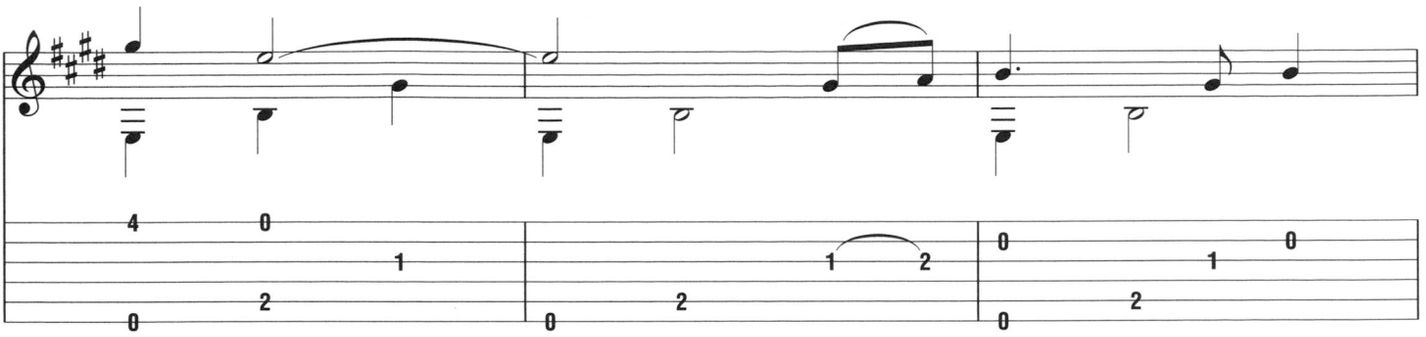

¢IV
CIV

CII
1.

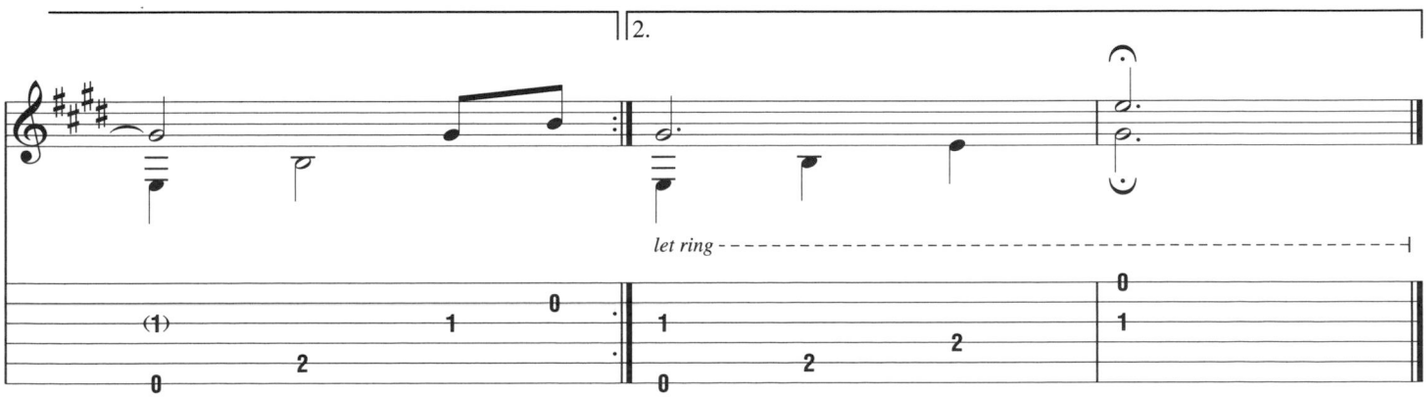
2.
let ring

Villanesca

By Enrique Granados

This Arrangement Copyright © 2008 Cherry Lane Music Company
International Copyright Secured All Rights Reserved

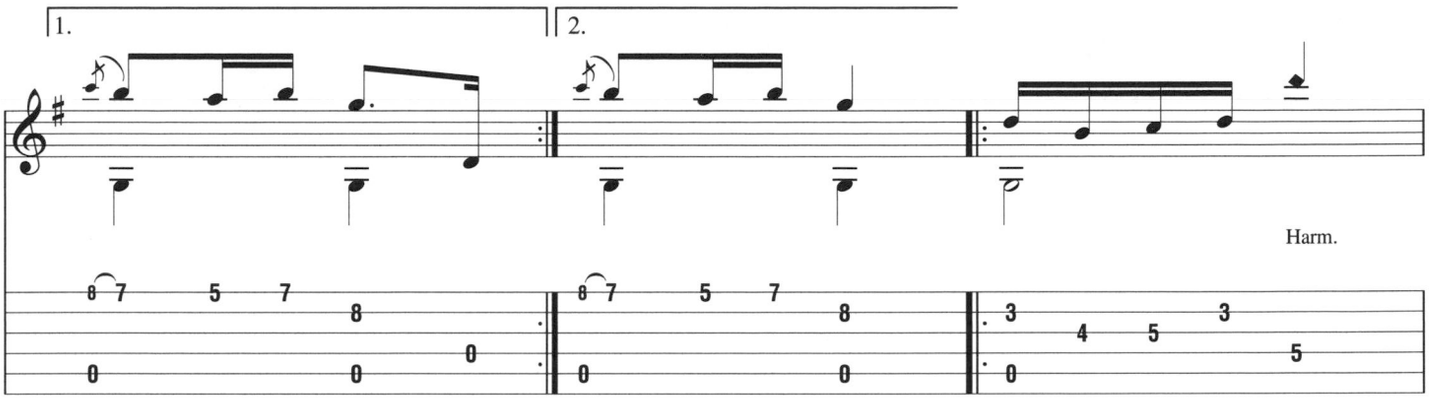
1.
2.
Harm.

1.
Harm.

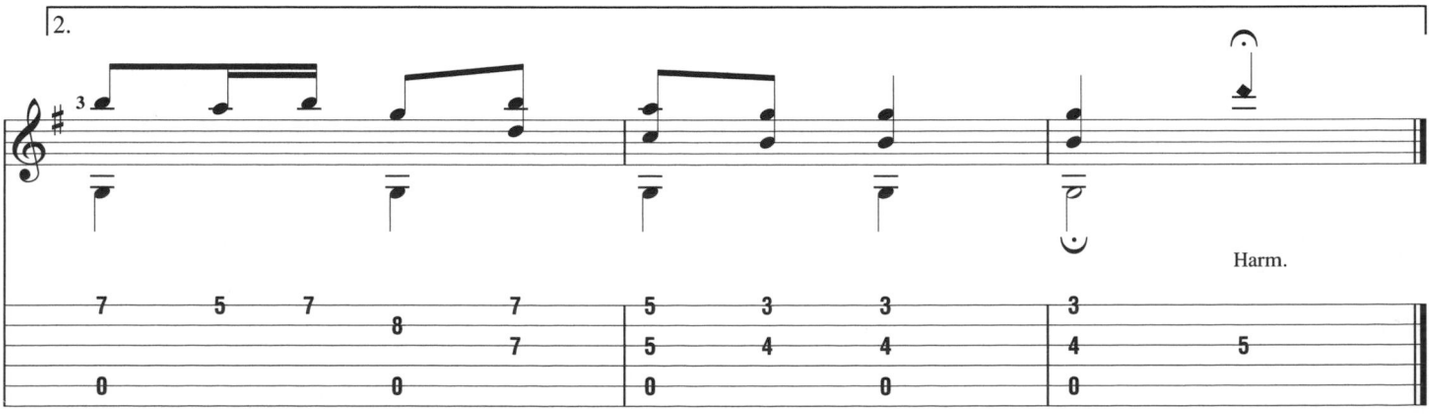
2.
Harm.

FINGERPICKING GUITAR BOOKS

Hone your fingerpicking skills with these great songbooks featuring solo guitar arrangements in standard notation and tablature. The arrangements in these books are carefully written for intermediate-level guitarists. Each song combines melody and harmony in one superb guitar fingerpicking arrangement. Each book also includes an introduction to basic fingerstyle guitar.

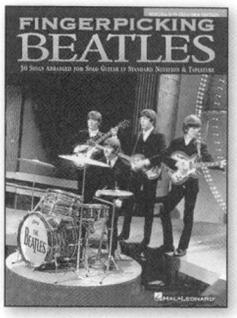

Fingerpicking Acoustic
00699614 15 songs..... $14.99

Fingerpicking Acoustic Classics
00160211 15 songs..... $16.99

Fingerpicking Acoustic Hits
00160202 15 songs..... $12.99

Fingerpicking Acoustic Rock
00699764 14 songs..... $14.99

Fingerpicking Ballads
00699717 15 songs..... $14.99

Fingerpicking Beatles
00699049 30 songs..... $24.99

Fingerpicking Beethoven
00702390 15 pieces..... $10.99

Fingerpicking Blues
00701277 15 songs $10.99

Fingerpicking Broadway Favorites
00699843 15 songs..... $9.99

Fingerpicking Broadway Hits
00699838 15 songs..... $7.99

Fingerpicking Campfire
00275964 15 songs..... $12.99

Fingerpicking Celtic Folk
00701148 15 songs..... $10.99

Fingerpicking Children's Songs
00699712 15 songs..... $9.99

Fingerpicking Christian
00701076 15 songs..... $12.99

Fingerpicking Christmas
00699599 20 carols..... $10.99

Fingerpicking Christmas Classics
00701695 15 songs..... $7.99

Fingerpicking Christmas Songs
00171333 15 songs..... $10.99

Fingerpicking Classical
00699620 15 pieces..... $10.99

Fingerpicking Country
00699687 17 songs..... $12.99

Fingerpicking Disney
00699711 15 songs..... $16.99

Fingerpicking Early Jazz Standards
00276565 15 songs $12.99

Fingerpicking Duke Ellington
00699845 15 songs..... $9.99

Fingerpicking Enya
00701161 15 songs..... $16.99

Fingerpicking Film Score Music
00160143 15 songs..... $12.99

Fingerpicking Gospel
00701059 15 songs..... $9.99

Fingerpicking Hit Songs
00160195 15 songs..... $12.99

Fingerpicking Hymns
00699688 15 hymns $12.99

Fingerpicking Irish Songs
00701965 15 songs..... $10.99

Fingerpicking Italian Songs
00159778 15 songs..... $12.99

Fingerpicking Jazz Favorites
00699844 15 songs..... $12.99

Fingerpicking Jazz Standards
00699840 15 songs..... $10.99

Fingerpicking Elton John
00237495 15 songs..... $14.99

Fingerpicking Latin Favorites
00699842 15 songs..... $12.99

Fingerpicking Latin Standards
00699837 15 songs..... $15.99

Fingerpicking Andrew Lloyd Webber
00699839 14 songs..... $16.99

Fingerpicking Love Songs
00699841 15 songs..... $14.99

Fingerpicking Love Standards
00699836 15 songs $9.99

Fingerpicking Lullabyes
00701276 16 songs..... $9.99

Fingerpicking Movie Music
00699919 15 songs..... $14.99

Fingerpicking Mozart
00699794 15 pieces..... $9.99

Fingerpicking Pop
00699615 15 songs..... $14.99

Fingerpicking Popular Hits
00139079 14 songs..... $12.99

Fingerpicking Praise
00699714 15 songs..... $14.99

Fingerpicking Rock
00699716 15 songs..... $14.99

Fingerpicking Standards
00699613 17 songs..... $14.99

Fingerpicking Wedding
00699637 15 songs..... $10.99

Fingerpicking Worship
00700554 15 songs..... $14.99

Fingerpicking Neil Young – Greatest Hits
00700134 16 songs..... $16.99

Fingerpicking Yuletide
00699654 16 songs..... $12.99

HAL•LEONARD®

Order these and more great publications from your favorite music retailer at
halleonard.com

Prices, contents and availability subject to change without notice.

0122
279